59 PIANO SOLOS

You Like to Play

ED. 1569

G. SCHIRMER, *Inc.*

DISTRIBUTED BY

HAL•LEONARD®
CORPORATION

7777 W. BLUEMOUND RD. P.O. BOX 13819 MILWAUKEE, WI 53213

CONTENTS

Tango in D

Edited by Carl Deis

Isaac Albeniz, Op. 165, No. 2

Printed in the U. S. A.

37186

6
Solfeggietto*)

Revised and fingered, with exact pedal signs,
and arranged for LEFT HAND SOLO *ad libit.*
by A. R. PARSONS

Carl Philipp Emanuel Bach

*) When the Solfeggietto is played with the left hand alone, the player's seat should be precisely in front of the twice-marked

$\bar{\bar{c}}$ of the pianoforte *clavier* (so-called "keyboard") viz:

37186

87186

10
Prelude
(Nº 1, from Well-tempered Clavichord)

J. S. BACH

Allegro (♩=112)

Piano

12
Prelude

J. S. Bach

Andante sostenuto. (♩ = 92.)

Six Variations.

on the Duet

Nel cor più non mi sento

from the Opera: **La Molinara** by **Paisiello**

Edited and fingered by
SIGMUND LEBERT

L. van BEETHOVEN

(a) Always strike the **appoggiatura-note** simultaneously with the first accompaniment - note, somewhat shortly, yet without impairing clearness. The accent falls, however, not on the appoggiatura, but on the principal note.

(b) The alterations given by us in small notes, aim at making these variations easily playable by small hands, which cannot yet stretch an octave.

(c) Continue from this movement to the following without interruption of the measure, except when the contrary is indicated by a fermata over the closing double-bar.

Var. I.

(a) Such a comma indicates a breaking-off somewhat sooner, and a subsequent fresh attack.

(b)

Var. III.

(a) Emphasize the left hand somewhat here, as it has the principal notes of the melody.

(b) Small hands must leave out the lowest tone.

Poco più tranquillo. (♪=144)

Var. IV.

(a) Both the *d-b* in the left hand, as also the *g* in the right are to be held during the execution of the small notes.

(a) *mp* (*mezzo piano*, rather softly) signifies a degree of tone-power between *p* and *mf*

Minuet in G

Edited and fingered by
Carl Deis

L. van Beethoven

Allegretto (♩=120)

Piano

Hungarian Dance, No. 5

Revised and fingered by
Wm. Scharfenberg

Johannes Brahms

Waltz

Edited by Carl Deis

Johannes Brahms. Op. 39, No. 15

Scarf-Dance
Der Schärpentanz
Scène de Ballet

Revised and fingered by
Wm Scharfenberg

C. CHAMINADE

Allegro. (♩ = 54)

Piano

p legato

cresc.

dim. — *p* *p* *p poco rubato*

cresc. *f*

dim. *p* *p*

Two Preludes

Edited and fingered by
Carl Deis

F. Chopin. Op. 28, No. 7

Andantino (♩=72 *senza rigore*)

Piano

p dolce

Ped.

Largo (♩=44 *giusto*)

Op. 28, No. 20

ff

Ped. *Ped.* *Ped.* *Ped.* *Ped.* *Ped.* *simile*

riten.

p

pp

cresc.

Ped.

A Madame la Comtesse Delphine Potocka

Valse

Revised and fingered by
Rafael Joseffy

F. Chopin. Op. 64, No. 1

Molto vivace

à Monsieur Johns de la Nouvelle-Orléans

Mazurka

Revised and fingered by
Rafael Joseffy

F. Chopin. Op. 7, No. 1

Ped. simile

Ped. simile

Ped. come sopra

Polonaise

à Mr J. FONTANA.

F. CHOPIN. Op. 40, No 1.

Allegro con brio.

Orientale

César Cui. Op. 50, No. 9
Transcribed by Carl Deis

49

Humoreske

Edited and fingered by
Louis Oesterle

Anton Dvořák. Op. 101, N⁰ 7

Poco lento e grazioso (♩=72)

Piano

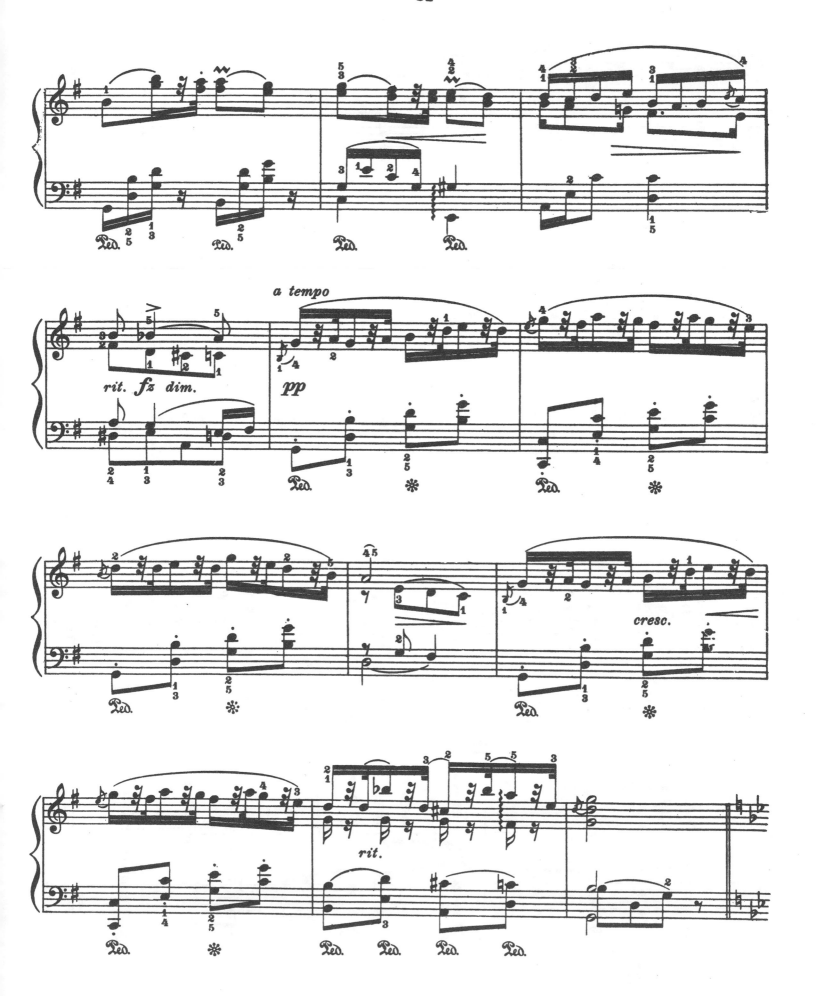

Original ✻

Salut d'amour
Love's Greeting

Edited and fingered by
Louis Oesterle

Edward Elgar. Op.12

Poem

Zdenko Fibich
Transcribed by Erno Rapée

Chanson

Rudolf Friml

A Alfredo G. Faria

Spanish Dance
Playera

Enrique Granados, Op. 5, No. 5

Album-Leaf
Albumblatt

Revised and fingered by W.S.

Edvard Grieg

Anitra's Tanz.
(Dance of Anitra.)

Edited and fingered by
Louis Oesterle.

EDVARD GRIEG. Op. 46, № 3.

Tempo di Mazurka. (♩=160.)

*) Trills without afterbeat.

An den Frühling.

(To Spring.)

Edited and fingered by
Louis Oesterle.

Allegro appassionato. (♩. = 84)

EDVARD GRIEG. Op. 43, № 6.

Zug der Zwerge.

(March of the Dwarfs.)

Edited and fingered by
Louis Oesterle.

EDVARD GRIEG. Op. 54, № 3.

Largo
from the Opera "Xerxes"

Edited by Carl Deis

George Frideric Handel

Crescendo.

Revised and fingered by
Wm Scharfenberg.

PER LASSON.

Allegretto.

Piano.

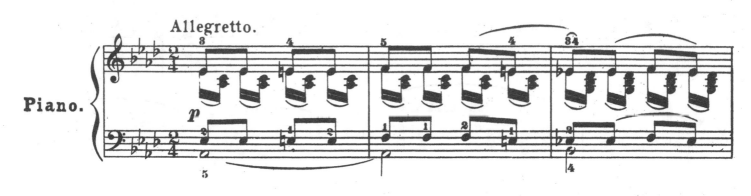

Consolation

Edited and fingered by
Rafael Joseffy

Franz Liszt

Liebestraum.
(A DREAM OF LOVE.)
Nocturne.

Edited and fingered by
E. PAUER.

FRANZ LISZT. (1811_1886.)

Poco Allegro, con affetto.

Piano.

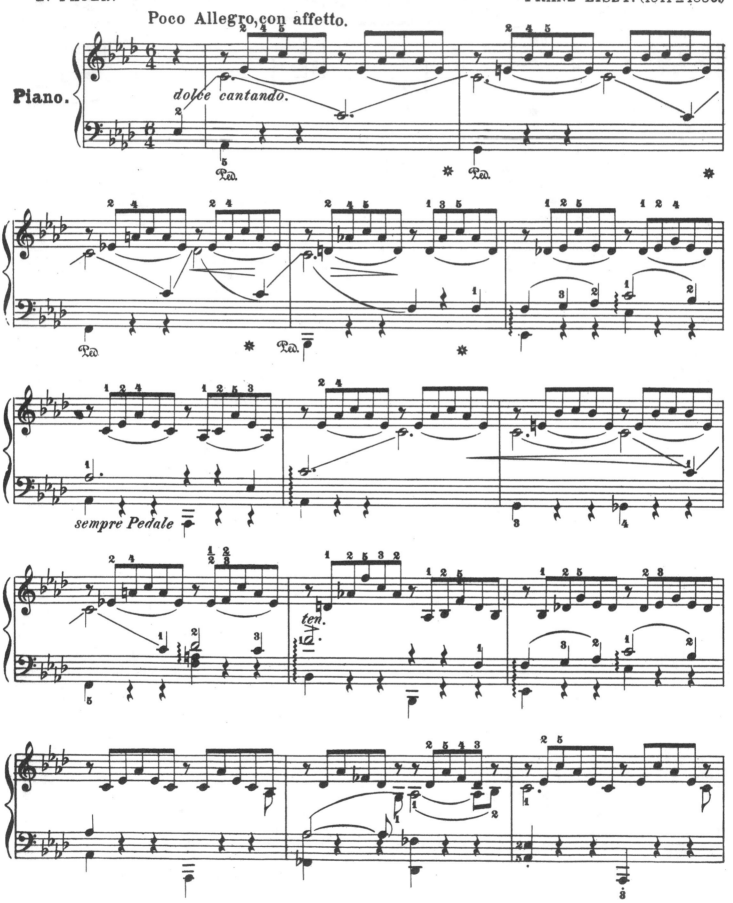

P. Mascagni

Cavalleria rusticana

Intermezzo sinfonico

P. Mascagni,
arr. by Max Spicker

Mélodie
Élégie

Edited and fingered by
LOUIS OESTERLE

Jules Massenet. Op. 10

Lento, ma non troppo

Piano

100
Spring-Song

Allegretto grazioso (♩ = 88)

Felix Mendelssohn, Op. 62, No. 6

a) The letters *o.* and *u.* indicate where the left hand is best placed over (*o.*) and under (*u.*) the right.

Venetian Boat-Song No.1

Felix Mendelssohn, Op. 19, No. 6

106
Consolation

Felix Mendelssohn,
Op. 30, No. 8

Adagio non troppo (♩=58)

Serenata

Revised and fingered by
Wm Scharfenberg

M. MOSZKOWSKI. Op.15, № 1

Andante grazioso

110 Rondo

Alla turca
Allegretto (♩ = 126)

W. A. MOZART

a) (ornament notation)

b) Play the first A in the bass with the C sharp in the
right hand.

a) Play the four notes in either hand simultaneously.

Barcarolle

Intermezzo from the opera "Les Contes d'Hoffmann"

J. Offenbach

May Night

Selim Palmgren, Op. 27, No. 4

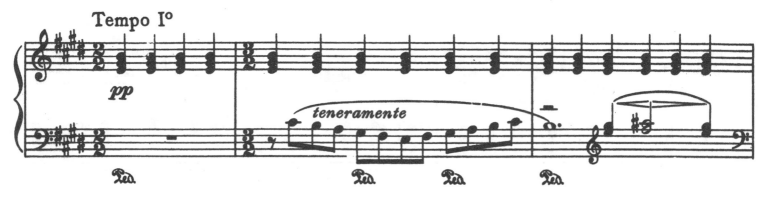

Prélude

Edited and fingered by
Louis Oesterle

(Andante)

S. RACHMANINOFF. Op. 3, № 2

Piano

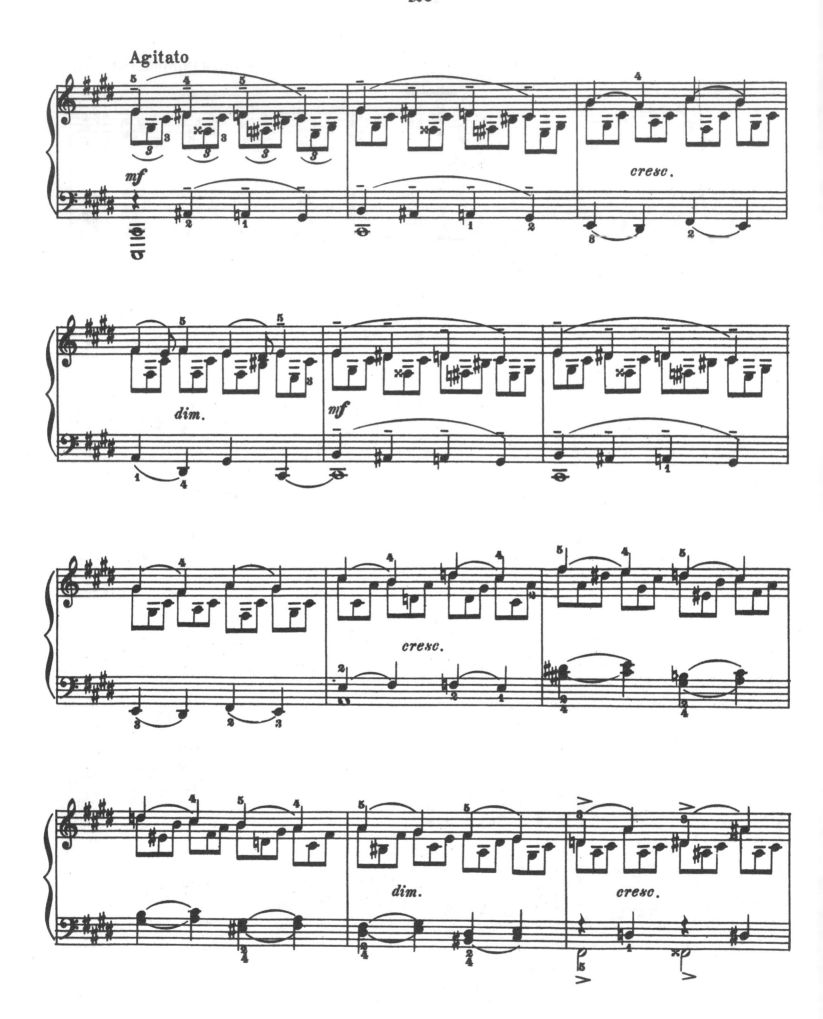

A Monsieur A. Siloti

Prélude

Edited and fingered by
Louis Oesterle

S. Rachmaninoff. Op. 23, № 5

Alla marcia (♩ = 108)

Piano

Un poco meno mosso

poco a poco accelerando e cresc. al Tempo I

Song of India

From the legend "Sadko"

Transcribed by Carl Deis

N. Rimsky-Korsakow

Kamennoi-Ostrow*

Revised by
Carl Deis

Anton Rubinstein, Op. 10, No. 22

Andante sostenuto ♩= 50

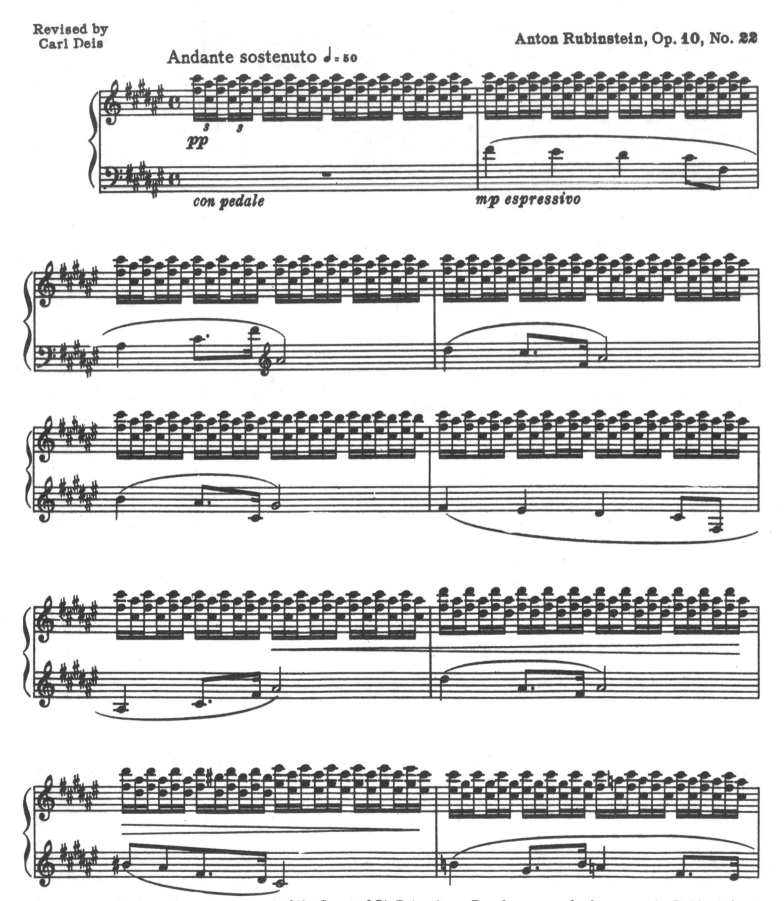

* The name of a favorite summer-resort of the Court of St. Petersburg, Russia, some of whose guests Rubinstein attempted to portray in the set of 24 pieces bearing the above title.

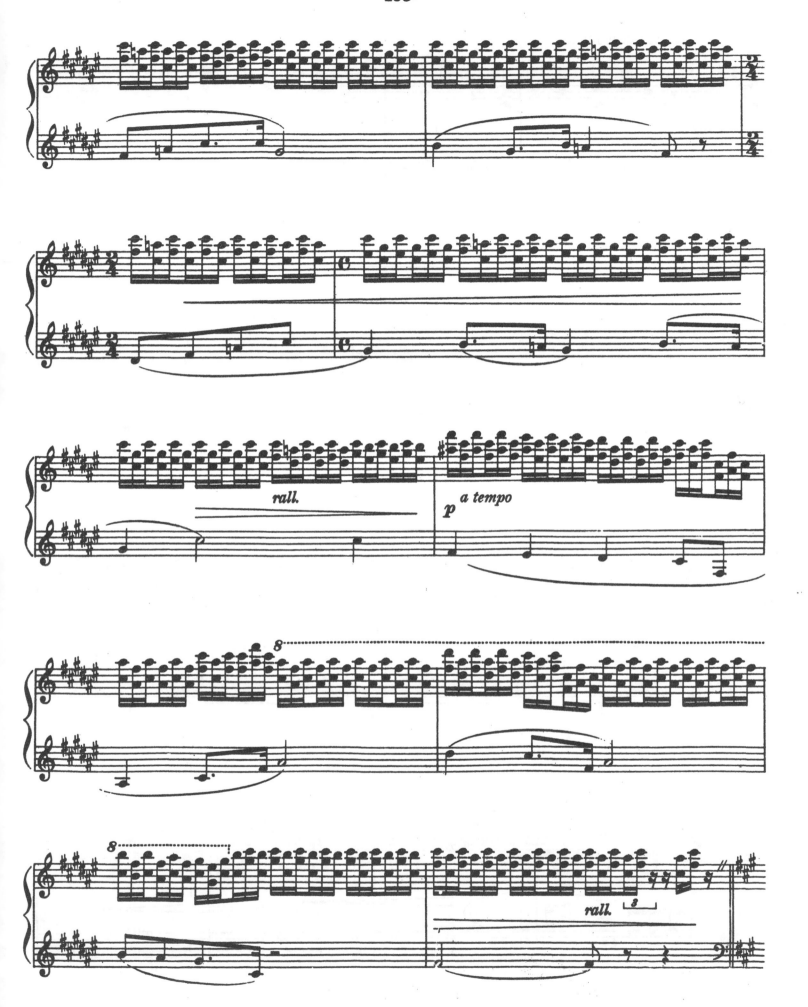

Mélodie

Edited and fingered
by Louis Oesterle

Anton Rubinstein. Op. 3, N⁰ 1

Tempo I.

The Swan

LE CYGNE

Melody from the "Carnaval des Animaux"

Camille Saint-Saëns

Edited and fingered by
Louis Oesterle

Transcribed by
E. Hoskier

Polish Dance

Edited by Carl Deis

Xaver Scharwenka

Military March

Edited and fingered by
Louis Oesterle

FRANZ SCHUBERT. Op. 51, N⁰ 1
Arr. by J. F. C. DIETRICH

Marcia D.C.

Moment Musical

Edited and fingered by
G. BUONAMICI

F. Schubert, Op. 94, No. 3

Allegro moderato (♩=96)

il basso sempre staccato

*) May also be
played thus:

Romance

Einfach.

Semplice. (♪ = 88)

Robert Schumann, Op. 28, No. 2

senza Pedale.

Träumerei

Robert Schumann, Op. 15, No. 7

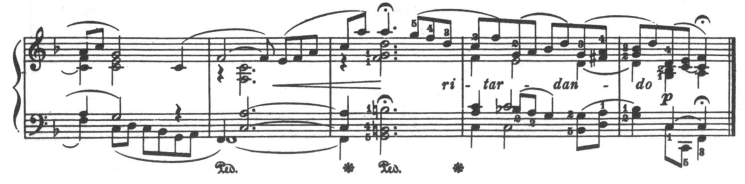

Romance

Jean Sibelius, Op. 24, No. 9

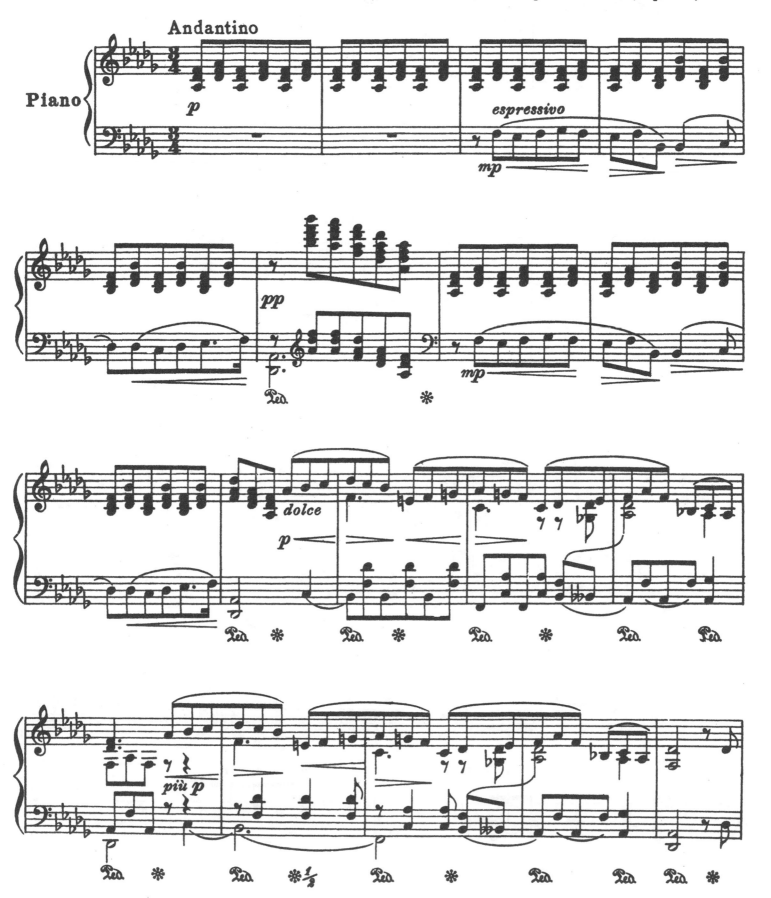

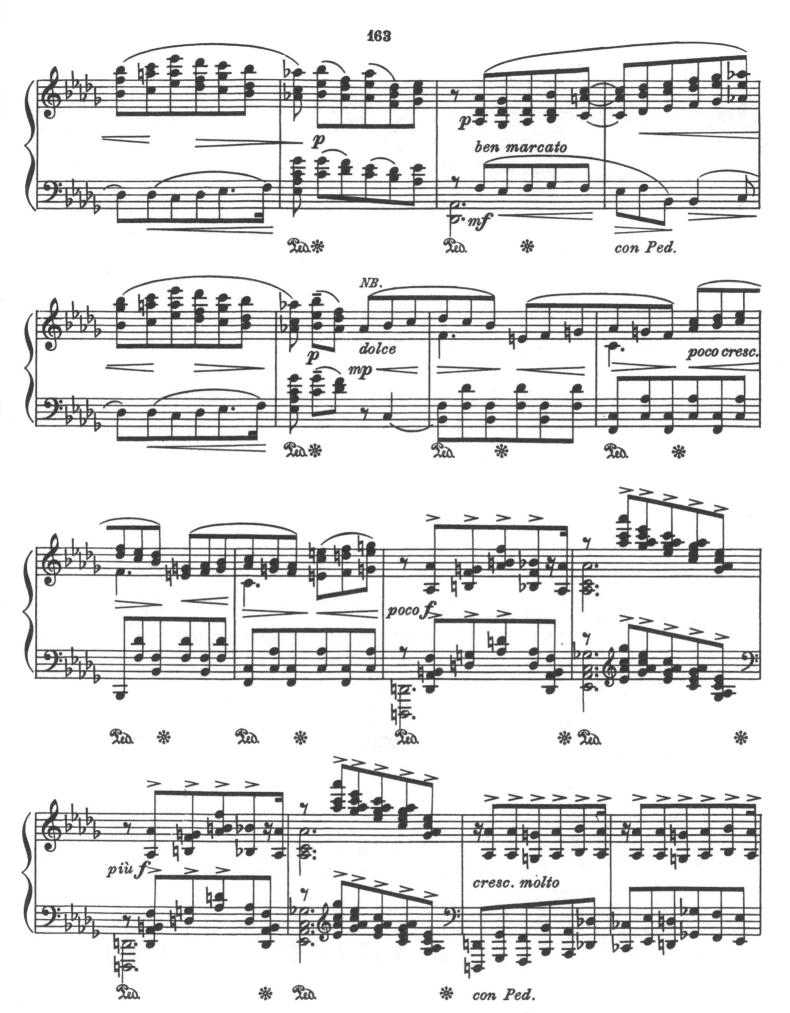

NB. If desired, a cut may be made from here to the point on the last page indicated by the sign ✛ .

Rustles of Spring
Frühlingsrauschen

Edited and fingered by
Louis Oesterle

CHRISTIAN SINDING
Op. 32, No 3

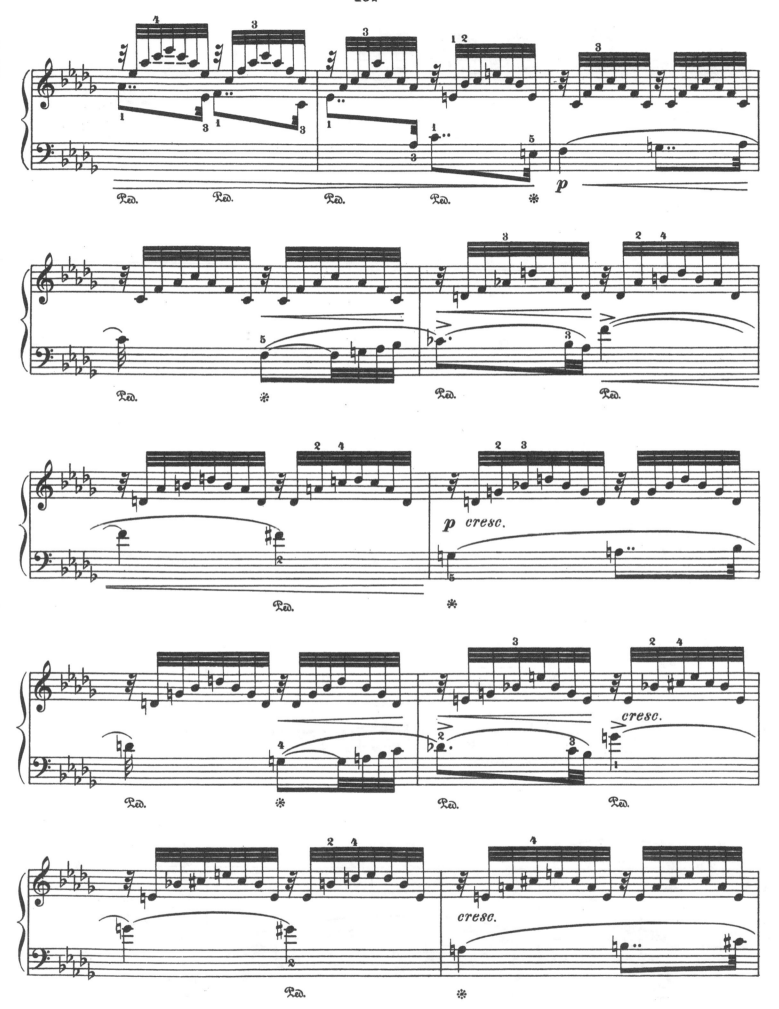

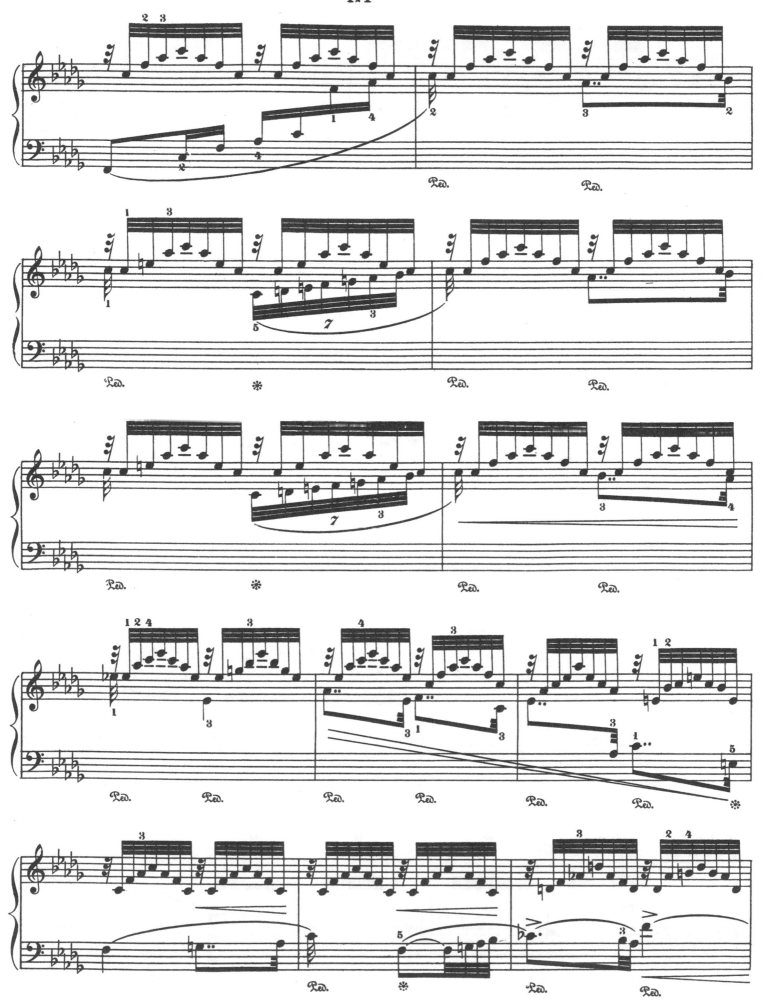

On the Beautiful Blue Danube

An der schönen blauen Donau

Johann Strauss. Op. 314

Waltz.

175

Dal Segno senza repetizione al Fine.

None but the lonely heart
Nur, wer die Sehnsucht kennt

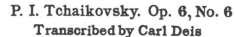

P. I. Tchaikovsky. Op. 6, No. 6
Transcribed by Carl Deis

Andante cantabile
from the Quartet Op. 11
by
P. TSCHAIKOWSKY

Edited and fingered by
Wm Scharfenberg

Transcribed by
Ch. Klindworth

la melodia molto espress.

Song without words

Chant sans paroles

Revised and fingered by
Wm Scharfenberg

P. TSCHAIKOWSKY

Allegretto grazioso e cantabile

Piano

Printed in the U.S.A.

Under the Leaves
Sous la feuillée

Revised and fingered by
Wm Scharfenberg.

FR. THOMÉ.

Poco agitato.

PIANO.

dolce

*ben marcato
il canto*

Y... ¿Como Le Vá?

Tango Argentino

On Motives by H. Herpin

J. Valverde

March from "Aïda"

GIUSEPPE VERDI

Allegro maestoso

R. Wagner
Lohengrin
Bridal Song

Revised and fingered by
Wᵐ Scharfenberg

Transcr. by S. JADASSOHN

Tannhäuser March

RICHARD WAGNER

Allegro